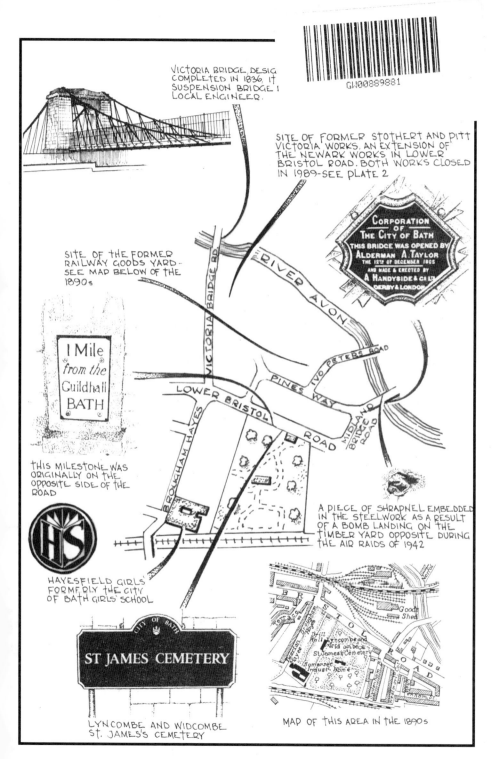

VICTORIA BRIDGE, DESIG
COMPLETED IN 1836, IT
SUSPENSION BRIDGE I
LOCAL ENGINEER.

SITE OF FORMER STOTHERT AND PITT
VICTORIA WORKS, AN EXTENSION OF
THE NEWARK WORKS IN LOWER
BRISTOL ROAD. BOTH WORKS CLOSED
IN 1989-SEE PLATE 2

SITE OF THE FORMER
RAILWAY GOODS YARD-
SEE MAP BELOW OF THE
1890s

CORPORATION
OF
THE CITY OF BATH
THIS BRIDGE WAS OPENED BY
ALDERMAN A. TAYLOR
THE 12TH OF DECEMBER 1905
AND MADE & ERECTED BY
A HANDYSIDE & Cº LTD
DERBY & LONDON

RIVER AVON

VICTORIA BRIDGE RD

IVO PETERS ROAD

PINES WAY

MIDLAND BRIDGE ROAD

LOWER BRISTOL ROAD

BROUGHAM HAYES

I Mile
from the
Guildhall
BATH

THIS MILESTONE WAS
ORIGINALLY ON THE
OPPOSITE SIDE OF THE
ROAD

A PIECE OF SHRAPNEL EMBEDDED
IN THE STEELWORK AS A RESULT
OF A BOMB LANDING ON THE
TIMBER YARD OPPOSITE DURING
THE AIR RAIDS OF 1942

HS

HAYESFIELD GIRLS'
FORMERLY THE CITY
OF BATH GIRLS' SCHOOL

CITY OF BATH
ST JAMES CEMETERY

BRISTOL ROAD

Goods
Shed

Drill
Hall
St James's Cemetery

Lyncombe and
Widcombe

Somerset
Indust. Home

LYNCOMBE AND WIDCOMBE
ST. JAMES'S CEMETERY

MAP OF THIS AREA IN THE 1890s

Plate 1

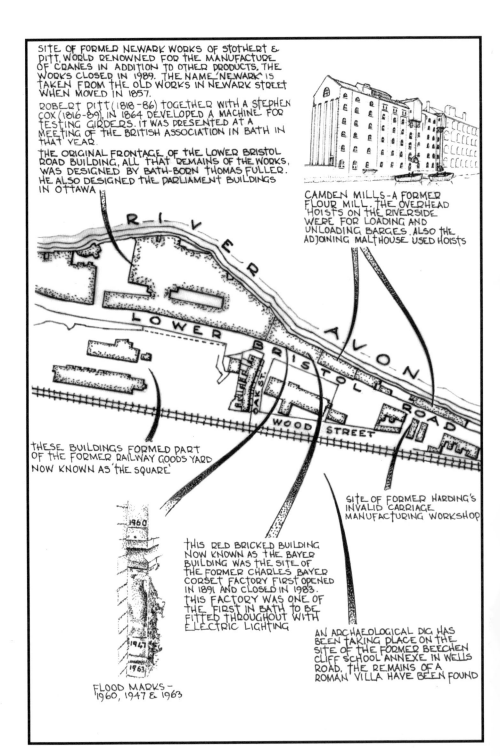

SITE OF FORMER NEWARK WORKS OF STOTHERT & PITT, WORLD RENOWNED FOR THE MANUFACTURE OF CRANES IN ADDITION TO OTHER PRODUCTS. THE WORKS CLOSED IN 1989. THE NAME 'NEWARK' IS TAKEN FROM THE OLD WORKS IN NEWARK STREET WHEN MOVED IN 1857.
ROBERT PITT (1818-86) TOGETHER WITH A STEPHEN COX (1816-89), IN 1864 DEVELOPED A MACHINE FOR TESTING GIRDERS. IT WAS PRESENTED AT A MEETING OF THE BRITISH ASSOCIATION IN BATH IN THAT YEAR.
THE ORIGINAL FRONTAGE OF THE LOWER BRISTOL ROAD BUILDING, ALL THAT REMAINS OF THE WORKS, WAS DESIGNED BY BATH-BORN THOMAS FULLER. HE ALSO DESIGNED THE PARLIAMENT BUILDINGS IN OTTAWA

CAMDEN MILLS - A FORMER FLOUR MILL. THE OVERHEAD HOISTS ON THE RIVERSIDE WERE FOR LOADING AND UNLOADING BARGES. ALSO THE ADJOINING MALTHOUSE USED HOISTS

RIVER

LOWER BRISTOL ROAD

AVON

OAK ST.

WOOD STREET

THESE BUILDINGS FORMED PART OF THE FORMER RAILWAY GOODS YARD NOW KNOWN AS 'THE SQUARE'

SITE OF FORMER HARDING'S INVALID CARRIAGE MANUFACTURING WORKSHOP

1960

THIS RED BRICKED BUILDING NOW KNOWN AS THE BAYER BUILDING WAS THE SITE OF THE FORMER CHARLES BAYER CORSET FACTORY FIRST OPENED IN 1891 AND CLOSED IN 1983. THIS FACTORY WAS ONE OF THE FIRST IN BATH TO BE FITTED THROUGHOUT WITH ELECTRIC LIGHTING

1947

1963

AN ARCHAEOLOGICAL DIG HAS BEEN TAKING PLACE ON THE SITE OF THE FORMER BEECHEN CLIFF SCHOOL ANNEXE IN WELLS ROAD. THE REMAINS OF A ROMAN VILLA HAVE BEEN FOUND

FLOOD MARKS - 1960, 1947 & 1963

Plate 2

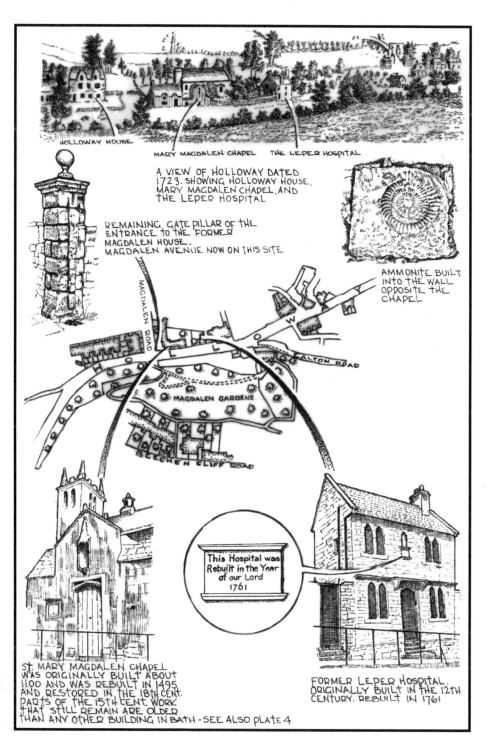

HOLLOWAY HOUSE   MARY MAGDALEN CHAPEL   THE LEPER HOSPITAL

A VIEW OF HOLLOWAY DATED 1723. SHOWING HOLLOWAY HOUSE, MARY MAGDALEN CHAPEL, AND THE LEPER HOSPITAL

REMAINING GATE PILLAR OF THE ENTRANCE TO THE FORMER MAGDALEN HOUSE. MAGDALEN AVENUE NOW ON THIS SITE

AMMONITE BUILT INTO THE WALL OPPOSITE THE CHAPEL

MAGDALEN ROAD

WELLS ROAD

ALTON ROAD

HOLLOWAY

MAGDALEN GARDENS

BEECHEN CLIFF ROAD

This Hospital was Rebuilt in the Year of our Lord 1761

ST. MARY MAGDALEN CHAPEL WAS ORIGINALLY BUILT ABOUT 1100 AND WAS REBUILT IN 1495 AND RESTORED IN THE 18TH CENT. PARTS OF THE 15TH CENT. WORK THAT STILL REMAIN ARE OLDER THAN ANY OTHER BUILDING IN BATH - SEE ALSO PLATE 4

FORMER LEPER HOSPITAL, ORIGINALLY BUILT IN THE 12TH CENTURY, REBUILT IN 1761

Plate 3

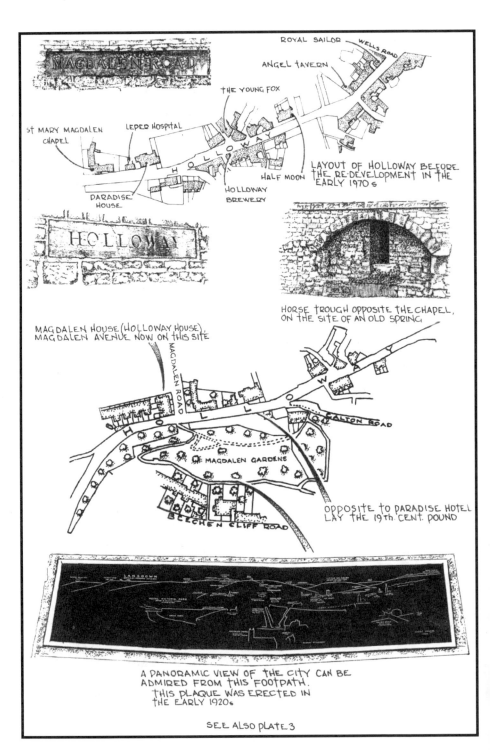

MAGDALEN ROAD

ROYAL SAILOR — WELLS ROAD
ANGEL TAVERN
THE YOUNG FOX
LEPER HOSPITAL
St MARY MAGDALEN CHAPEL
HALF MOON
HOLLOWAY BREWERY
PARADISE HOUSE

LAYOUT OF HOLLOWAY BEFORE THE RE-DEVELOPMENT IN THE EARLY 1970s

HOLLOWAY

HORSE TROUGH OPPOSITE THE CHAPEL, ON THE SITE OF AN OLD SPRING

MAGDALEN HOUSE (HOLLOWAY HOUSE), MAGDALEN AVENUE NOW ON THIS SITE

MAGDALEN ROAD

ALTON ROAD

MAGDALEN GARDENS

BEECHEN CLIFF ROAD

OPPOSITE TO PARADISE HOTEL LAY THE 19th. CENT. POUND

LANSDOWN

A PANORAMIC VIEW OF THE CITY CAN BE ADMIRED FROM THIS FOOTPATH.
THIS PLAQUE WAS ERECTED IN THE EARLY 1920s

SEE ALSO PLATE 3

Plate 4

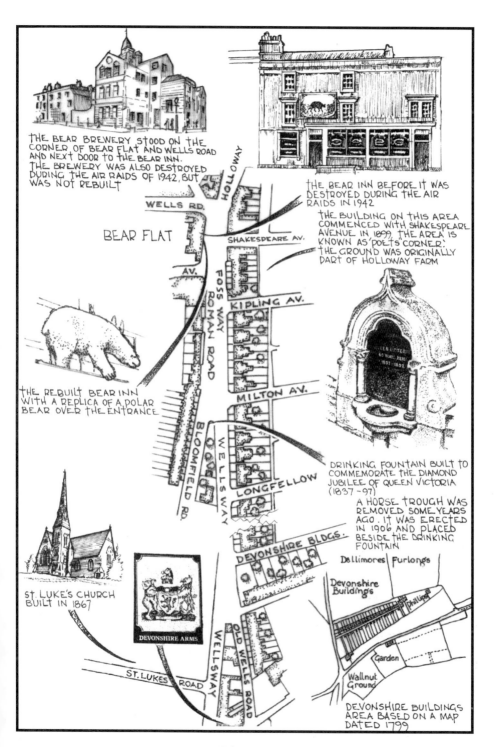

THE BEAR BREWERY STOOD ON THE CORNER OF BEAR FLAT AND WELLS ROAD AND NEXT DOOR TO THE BEAR INN. THE BREWERY WAS ALSO DESTROYED DURING THE AIR RAIDS OF 1942, BUT WAS NOT REBUILT

HOLLOWAY

WELLS RD.

BEAR FLAT

SHAKESPEARE AV.

THE BEAR INN BEFORE IT WAS DESTROYED DURING THE AIR RAIDS IN 1942

THE BUILDING ON THIS AREA COMMENCED WITH SHAKESPEARE AVENUE IN 1899, THE AREA IS KNOWN AS 'POETS CORNER'. THE GROUND WAS ORIGINALLY PART OF HOLLOWAY FARM

AV.

FOSS WAY ROMAN ROAD

KIPLING AV.

MILTON AV.

THE REBUILT BEAR INN WITH A REPLICA OF A POLAR BEAR OVER THE ENTRANCE

BLOOMFIELD RD.

WELLS WAY

LONGFELLOW

DRINKING FOUNTAIN BUILT TO COMMEMORATE THE DIAMOND JUBILEE OF QUEEN VICTORIA (1837-97)

A HORSE TROUGH WAS REMOVED SOME YEARS AGO. IT WAS ERECTED IN 1906 AND PLACED BESIDE THE DRINKING FOUNTAIN

DEVONSHIRE BLDGS.

Dellimores Furlongs

Devonshire Buildings

Phillips

ST. LUKE'S CHURCH BUILT IN 1867

DEVONSHIRE ARMS

WELLSWAY

OLD WELLS ROAD

Garden

Wallnut Ground

ST. LUKES ROAD

DEVONSHIRE BUILDINGS AREA BASED ON A MAP DATED 1799

Plate 5

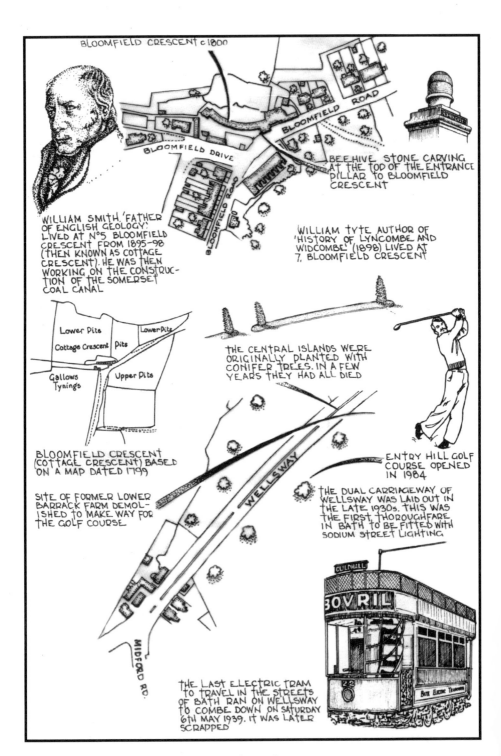

BLOOMFIELD CRESCENT c 1800

BLOOMFIELD ROAD

BLOOMFIELD DRIVE

BLOOMFIELD ROAD

BEEHIVE STONE CARVING AT THE TOP OF THE ENTRANCE PILLAR TO BLOOMFIELD CRESCENT

WILLIAM SMITH. 'FATHER OF ENGLISH GEOLOGY'. LIVED AT N°5 BLOOMFIELD CRESCENT FROM 1895-98 (THEN KNOWN AS COTTAGE CRESCENT). HE WAS THEN WORKING ON THE CONSTRUCTION OF THE SOMERSET COAL CANAL

WILLIAM TYTE AUTHOR OF 'HISTORY OF LYNCOMBE AND WIDCOMBE' (1898) LIVED AT 7, BLOOMFIELD CRESCENT

Lower Pits

Lower Pits

Cottage Crescent Pits

Gallows Tynings

Upper Pits

THE CENTRAL ISLANDS WERE ORIGINALLY PLANTED WITH CONIFER TREES. IN A FEW YEARS THEY HAD ALL DIED

BLOOMFIELD CRESCENT (COTTAGE CRESCENT) BASED ON A MAP DATED 1799

ENTRY HILL GOLF COURSE OPENED IN 1984

WELLSWAY

SITE OF FORMER LOWER BARRACK FARM DEMOLISHED TO MAKE WAY FOR THE GOLF COURSE

THE DUAL CARRIAGEWAY OF WELLSWAY WAS LAID OUT IN THE LATE 1930s. THIS WAS THE FIRST THOROUGHFARE IN BATH TO BE FITTED WITH SODIUM STREET LIGHTING

MIDFORD RD.

GUILDHALL

BOVRIL

BATH ELECTRIC TRAMWAYS

THE LAST ELECTRIC TRAM TO TRAVEL IN THE STREETS OF BATH RAN ON WELLSWAY TO COMBE DOWN ON SATURDAY 6TH MAY 1939. IT WAS LATER SCRAPPED

Plate 6

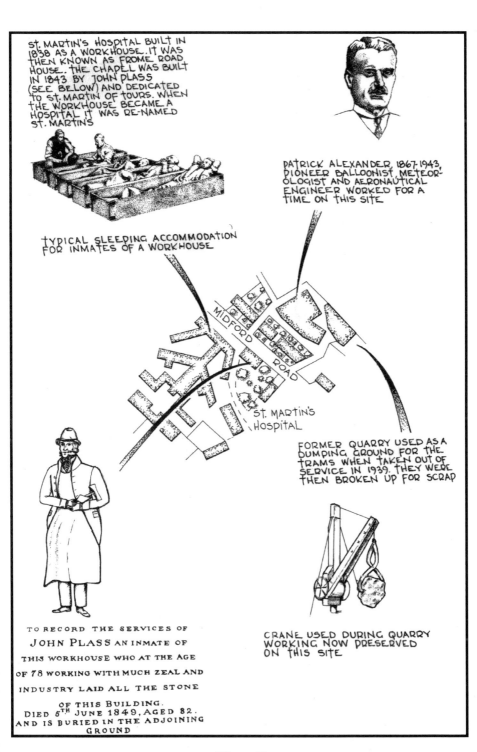

ST. MARTIN'S HOSPITAL BUILT IN 1838 AS A WORKHOUSE. IT WAS THEN KNOWN AS FROME ROAD HOUSE. THE CHAPEL WAS BUILT IN 1843 BY JOHN PLASS (SEE BELOW) AND DEDICATED TO ST. MARTIN OF TOURS. WHEN THE WORKHOUSE BECAME A HOSPITAL IT WAS RE-NAMED ST. MARTINS

TYPICAL SLEEPING ACCOMMODATION FOR INMATES OF A WORKHOUSE

PATRICK ALEXANDER, 1867-1943, PIONEER BALLOONIST, METEOROLOGIST AND AERONAUTICAL ENGINEER WORKED FOR A TIME ON THIS SITE

MIDFORD ROAD

ST. MARTIN'S HOSPITAL

FORMER QUARRY USED AS A DUMPING GROUND FOR THE TRAMS WHEN TAKEN OUT OF SERVICE IN 1939. THEY WERE THEN BROKEN UP FOR SCRAP

CRANE USED DURING QUARRY WORKING NOW PRESERVED ON THIS SITE

TO RECORD THE SERVICES OF JOHN PLASS AN INMATE OF THIS WORKHOUSE WHO AT THE AGE OF 78 WORKING WITH MUCH ZEAL AND INDUSTRY LAID ALL THE STONE OF THIS BUILDING. DIED 5TH JUNE 1849, AGED 82. AND IS BURIED IN THE ADJOINING GROUND

Plate 7

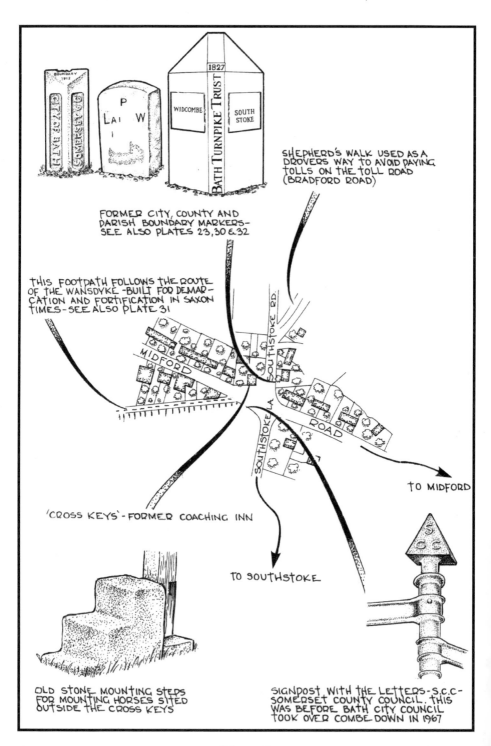

BOUNDARY 1912

P L A I W I

1827

WIDCOMBE   SOUTH STOKE

BATH TURNPIKE TRUST

FORMER CITY, COUNTY AND PARISH BOUNDARY MARKERS— SEE ALSO PLATES 23, 30 & 32

SHEPHERD'S WALK USED AS A DROVERS WAY TO AVOID PAYING TOLLS ON THE TOLL ROAD (BRADFORD ROAD)

THIS FOOTPATH FOLLOWS THE ROUTE OF THE WANSDYKE — BUILT FOR DEMARCATION AND FORTIFICATION IN SAXON TIMES — SEE ALSO PLATE 31

MIDFORD

SOUTHSTOKE RD.

SOUTHSTOKE LA.

ROAD

TO MIDFORD

'CROSS KEYS'— FORMER COACHING INN

TO SOUTHSTOKE

OLD STONE MOUNTING STEPS FOR MOUNTING HORSES SITED OUTSIDE THE CROSS KEYS

SIGNPOST WITH THE LETTERS — S.C.C — SOMERSET COUNTY COUNCIL. THIS WAS BEFORE BATH CITY COUNCIL TOOK OVER COMBE DOWN IN 1967

S C C

Plate 8

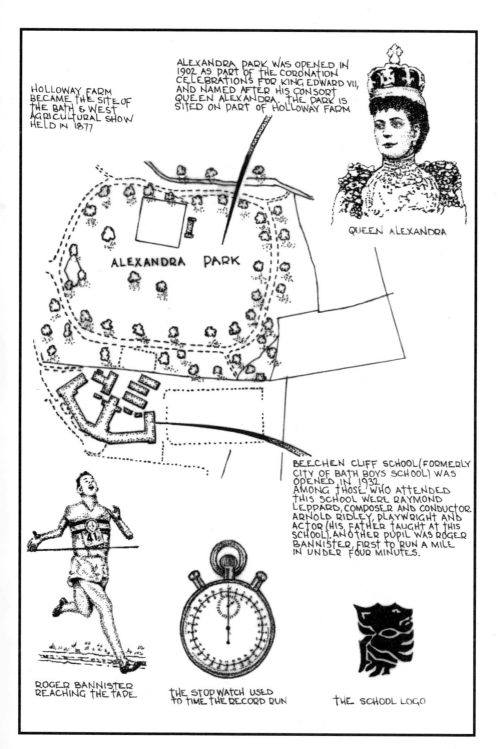

HOLLOWAY FARM BECAME THE SITE OF THE BATH & WEST AGRICULTURAL SHOW HELD IN 1877

ALEXANDRA PARK WAS OPENED IN 1902 AS PART OF THE CORONATION CELEBRATIONS FOR KING EDWARD VII, AND NAMED AFTER HIS CONSORT QUEEN ALEXANDRA. THE PARK IS SITED ON PART OF HOLLOWAY FARM

QUEEN ALEXANDRA

ALEXANDRA PARK

BEECHEN CLIFF SCHOOL (FORMERLY CITY OF BATH BOYS SCHOOL) WAS OPENED IN 1932. AMONG THOSE WHO ATTENDED THIS SCHOOL WERE RAYMOND LEPPARD, COMPOSER AND CONDUCTOR. ARNOLD RIDLEY, PLAYWRIGHT AND ACTOR (HIS FATHER TAUGHT AT THIS SCHOOL). ANOTHER PUPIL WAS ROGER BANNISTER, FIRST TO RUN A MILE IN UNDER FOUR MINUTES.

ROGER BANNISTER REACHING THE TAPE

THE STOPWATCH USED TO TIME THE RECORD RUN

THE SCHOOL LOGO

Plate 9

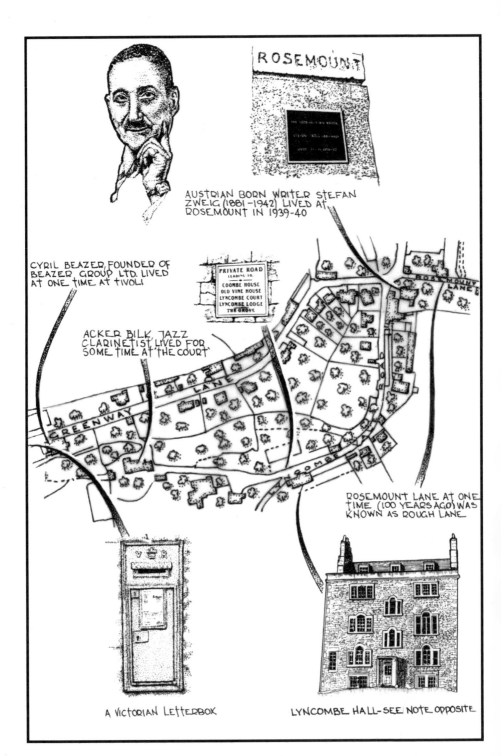

AUSTRIAN BORN WRITER STEFAN ZWEIG (1881-1942) LIVED AT ROSEMOUNT IN 1939-40

CYRIL BEAZER, FOUNDER OF BEAZER GROUP LTD. LIVED AT ONE TIME AT 'TIVOLI'

PRIVATE ROAD
LEADING TO.
COOMBE HOUSE
OLD VINE HOUSE
LYNCOMBE COURT
LYNCOMBE LODGE
THE GROVE

ACKER BILK, JAZZ CLARINETIST LIVED FOR SOME TIME AT 'THE COURT'

ROSEMOUNT LANE AT ONE TIME (100 YEARS AGO) WAS KNOWN AS ROUGH LANE

A VICTORIAN LETTERBOX

LYNCOMBE HALL-SEE NOTE OPPOSITE

Plate 10

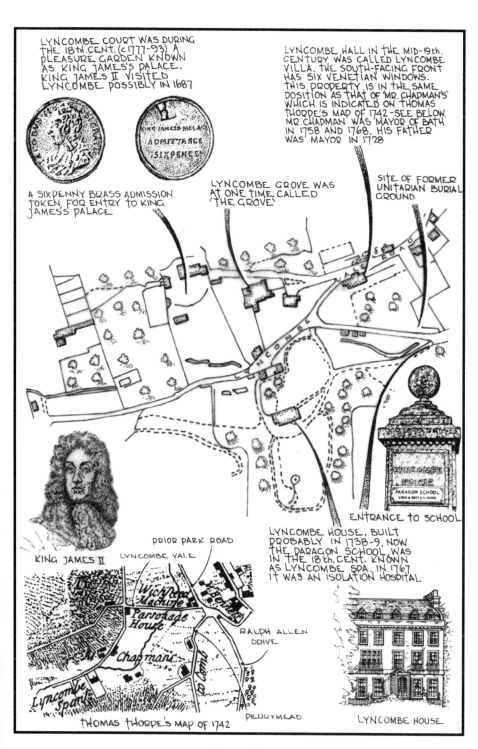

LYNCOMBE COURT WAS DURING THE 18th. CENT. (C1777-93) A PLEASURE GARDEN KNOWN AS KING JAMES'S PALACE. KING JAMES II VISITED LYNCOMBE POSSIBLY IN 1687

LYNCOMBE HALL IN THE MID-19th. CENTURY WAS CALLED LYNCOMBE VILLA. THE SOUTH-FACING FRONT HAS SIX VENETIAN WINDOWS. THIS PROPERTY IS IN THE SAME POSITION AS THAT OF 'MR. CHAPMAN'S' WHICH IS INDICATED ON THOMAS THORPE'S MAP OF 1742 - SEE BELOW. MR. CHAPMAN WAS MAYOR OF BATH IN 1758 AND 1768. HIS FATHER WAS MAYOR IN 1728

A SIXPENNY BRASS ADMISSION TOKEN FOR ENTRY TO KING JAMES'S PALACE

LYNCOMBE GROVE WAS AT ONE TIME CALLED 'THE GROVE'

SITE OF FORMER UNITARIAN BURIAL GROUND

ENTRANCE to SCHOOL

LYNCOMBE HOUSE, BUILT PROBABLY IN 1738-9, NOW THE PARAGON SCHOOL WAS IN THE 18th. CENT. KNOWN AS LYNCOMBE SPA, IN 1767 IT WAS AN ISOLATION HOSPITAL

KING JAMES II

THOMAS THORPE'S MAP OF 1742

LYNCOMBE HOUSE

Plate 11

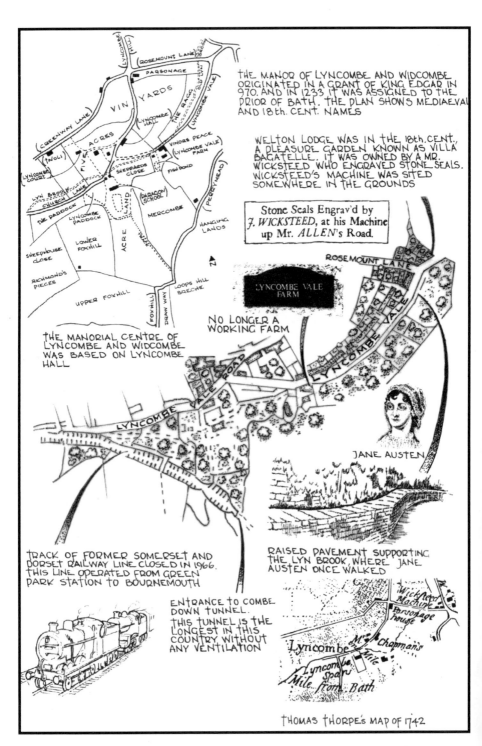

THE MANOR OF LYNCOMBE AND WIDCOMBE ORIGINATED IN A GRANT OF KING EDGAR IN 970. AND IN 1233 IT WAS ASSIGNED TO THE PRIOR OF BATH. THE PLAN SHOWS MEDIAEVAL AND 18th. CENT. NAMES

WELTON LODGE WAS IN THE 18th. CENT. A PLEASURE GARDEN KNOWN AS VILLA BAGATELLE. IT WAS OWNED BY A MR. WICKSTEED WHO ENGRAVED STONE SEALS. WICKSTEED'S MACHINE WAS SITED SOMEWHERE IN THE GROUNDS

Stone Seals Engrav'd by
J. WICKSTEED, at his Machine
up Mr. ALLEN's Road.

LYNCOMBE VALE FARM

NO LONGER A WORKING FARM

THE MANORIAL CENTRE OF LYNCOMBE AND WIDCOMBE WAS BASED ON LYNCOMBE HALL

JANE AUSTEN

TRACK OF FORMER SOMERSET AND DORSET RAILWAY LINE CLOSED IN 1966. THIS LINE OPERATED FROM GREEN PARK STATION TO BOURNEMOUTH

RAISED PAVEMENT SUPPORTING THE LYN BROOK, WHERE JANE AUSTEN ONCE WALKED

ENTRANCE TO COMBE DOWN TUNNEL. THIS TUNNEL IS THE LONGEST IN THIS COUNTRY WITHOUT ANY VENTILATION

THOMAS THORPE'S MAP OF 1742

Plate 12

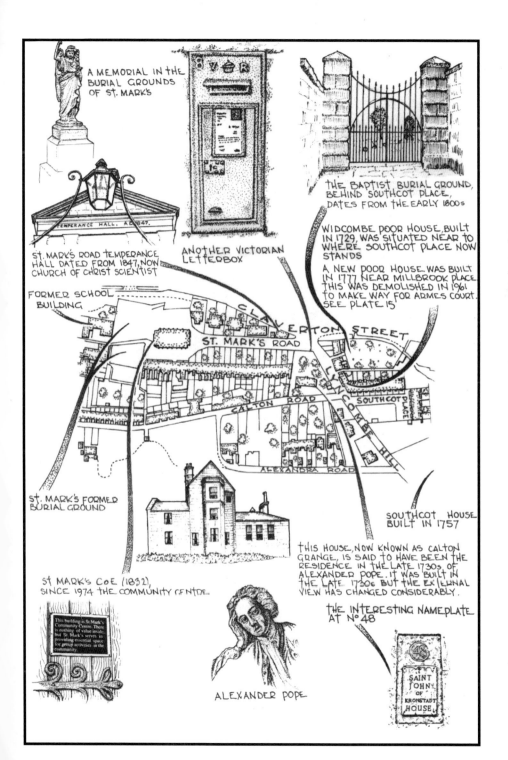

A MEMORIAL IN THE BURIAL GROUNDS OF ST. MARK'S

THE BAPTIST BURIAL GROUND, BEHIND SOUTHCOT PLACE, DATES FROM THE EARLY 1800s

ST. MARK'S ROAD TEMPERANCE HALL DATED FROM 1847, NOW CHURCH OF CHRIST SCIENTIST

ANOTHER VICTORIAN LETTERBOX

WIDCOMBE POOR HOUSE, BUILT IN 1729, WAS SITUATED NEAR TO WHERE SOUTHCOT PLACE NOW STANDS

A NEW POOR HOUSE WAS BUILT IN 1777 NEAR MILLBROOK PLACE THIS WAS DEMOLISHED IN 1961 TO MAKE WAY FOR ARMES COURT. SEE PLATE 15

FORMER SCHOOL BUILDING

CLAVERTON STREET

ST. MARK'S ROAD

LYNCOMBE HILL

SOUTHCOT PLACE

CALTON ROAD

ALEXANDRA ROAD

ST. MARK'S FORMER BURIAL GROUND

SOUTHCOT HOUSE BUILT IN 1757

THIS HOUSE, NOW KNOWN AS CALTON GRANGE, IS SAID TO HAVE BEEN THE RESIDENCE IN THE LATE 1730s OF ALEXANDER POPE. IT WAS BUILT IN THE LATE 1730s BUT THE EXTERNAL VIEW HAS CHANGED CONSIDERABLY.

St MARK'S CoE (1832), SINCE 1974 THE COMMUNITY CENTRE.

This building is St.Mark's Community Centre. There is nothing of value inside, but St. Mark's serves in providing essential space for group activities in the community.

ALEXANDER POPE

THE INTERESTING NAMEPLATE AT Nº 48

48 SAINT JOHN OF KRONSTADT HOUSE

Plate 13

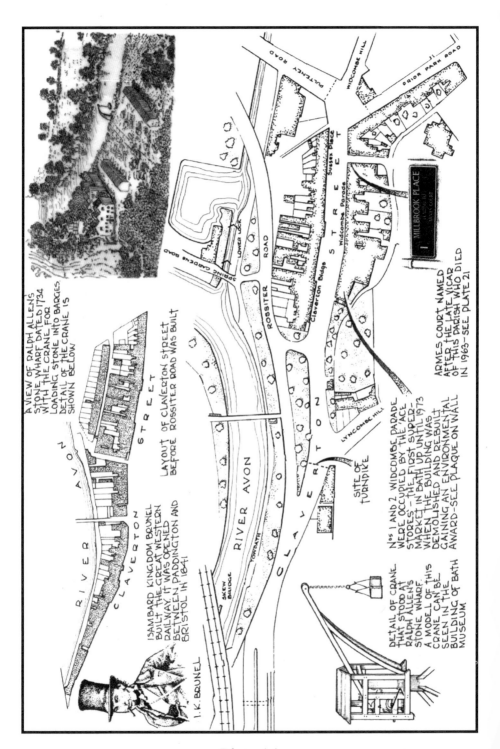

A VIEW OF RALPH ALLEN'S STONE WHARF DATED 1734 WITH THE CRANE FOR LOADING STONE INTO BARGES DETAIL OF THE CRANE IS SHOWN BELOW

LAYOUT OF CLAVERTON STREET BEFORE ROSSITER ROAD WAS BUILT

ISAMBARD KINGDOM BRUNEL BUILT THE GREAT WESTERN RAILWAY. IT WAS OPENED BETWEEN PADDINGTON AND BRISTOL IN 1841

I. K. BRUNEL

DETAIL OF CRANE THAT STOOD AT RALPH ALLEN'S STONE WHARF. A MODEL OF THIS CRANE CAN BE SEEN IN THE BUILDING OF BATH MUSEUM

Nos 1 AND 2 WIDCOMBE PARADE WERE OCCUPIED BY THE 'ACE STORES' - THE FIRST SUPER-MARKET IN BATH UP UNTIL 1973 WHEN THE BUILDING WAS DEMOLISHED AND REBUILT GAINING AN ENVIRONMENTAL AWARD - SEE PLATE 21

ARMES COURT NAMED AFTER THE LATE VICAR OF THIS PARISH WHO DIED IN 1963 - SEE PLATE 21

RIVER AVON

CLAVERTON STREET

RIVER AVON

CLAVERTON

SITE OF TURNPIKE

SKEW BRIDGE

TOWPATH

LYNCOMBE HILL

MILLBROOK PLACE

ARMES COURT

ROSSITER ROAD

SPRING GARDENS ROAD

LOWER LOCK

Claverton Bridge

Widcombe Parade

Sussex Place

SUSSEX STREET

PULTENEY ROAD

WIDCOMBE HILL

PRIOR PARK ROAD

Plate 14

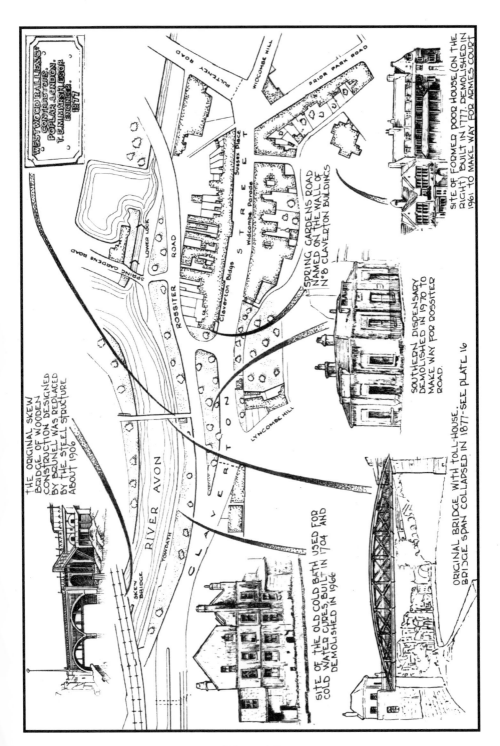

WESTWOOD BAILEY & CO.
CONTRACTORS,
POPLAR, LONDON.
T. EMMARSH, RESDT. ENGINEER
1877

SITE OF FORMER POOR HOUSE (ON THE RIGHT) BUILT IN 1777. DEMOLISHED IN 1961 TO MAKE WAY FOR ARMES COURT.

SPRING GARDENS ROAD NAMED ON THE WALL OF N°8 CLAVERTON BUILDINGS

SOUTHERN DISPENSARY DEMOLISHED IN 1970 TO MAKE WAY FOR ROSSITER ROAD.

THE ORIGINAL SKEW BRIDGE OF WOODEN CONSTRUCTION DESIGNED BY BRUNEL WAS REPLACED BY THE STEEL STRUCTURE ABOUT 1906

SITE OF THE OLD COLD BATH USED FOR COLD WATER CURES. BUILT IN 1704 AND DEMOLISHED IN 1906

ORIGINAL BRIDGE WITH TOLL-HOUSE. BRIDGE SPAN COLLAPSED IN 1877-SEE PLATE 16

RIVER AVON

TOWPATH

SKEW BRIDGE

C L A V E R T O N

PULTENEY ROAD

WIDCOMBE HILL

PRIOR PARK ROAD

S T R E E T

Sussex Place

Widcombe Parade

Claverton Bridge

LYNCOMBE HILL

SPRING GARDENS ROAD

ROSSITER ROAD

LOWER LOCK

Plate 15

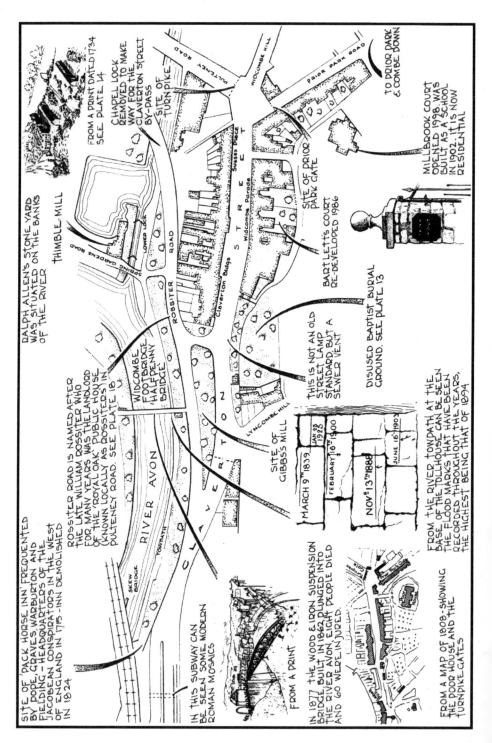

SITE OF 'PACK HORSE INN' FREQUENTED BY POPE, GRAVES, WARBURTON AND FIELDING. - HEADQUARTERS OF THE JACOBEAN CONSPIRATORS IN THE WEST OF ENGLAND IN 1715 - INN DEMOLISHED IN 1824

RALPH ALLEN'S STONE YARD WAS SITUATED ON THE BANKS OF THE RIVER

THIMBLE MILL

CHAPEL LOCK REMOVED TO MAKE WAY FOR THE CLAVERTON STREET BY-PASS

FROM A PRINT DATED 1734 SEE PLATE 14

TO PRIOR PARK & COMBE DOWN

MILLBROOK COURT OPENED 1998. WAS BUILT AS A SCHOOL IN 1902. IT IS NOW RESIDENTIAL

SITE OF TURNPIKE

ROSSITER ROAD IS NAMED AFTER THE LATE WILLIAM ROSSITER WHO FOR MANY YEARS WAS THE LANDLORD OF THE 'ROYAL OAK' PUBLIC HOUSE (KNOWN LOCALLY AS ROSSITER'S) IN PULTENEY ROAD. SEE PLATE 18

LOWER LOCK

SPRING GARDENS ROAD

ROSSITER ROAD

WIDCOMBE FOOTBRIDGE 'HALFPENNY BRIDGE'

RIVER AVON

TOWPATH

SKEW BRIDGE

IN THIS SUBWAY CAN BE SEEN SOME MODERN ROMAN MOSAICS

FROM A PRINT

IN 1877 THE WOOD & IRON SUSPENSION BRIDGE, BUILT IN 1862, PLUNGED INTO THE RIVER AVON. EIGHT PEOPLE DIED AND 60 WERE INJURED

CLAVERTON

Claverton Bridge

Sussex Place

Widcombe Parade

WIDCOMBE HILL

PULTENEY ROAD

STREET

SITE OF PRIOR PARK GATE

BARTLETT'S COURT RE-DEVELOPED 1986

LYNCOMBE HILL

SITE OF GIBBS'S MILL

THIS IS NOT AN OLD STREET LAMP STANDARD. BUT A SEWER VENT

DISUSED BAPTIST BURIAL GROUND. SEE PLATE 13

MARCH 9TH 1839

JAN 25 1925

FEBRUARY 16TH 1900

NOVR 13TH 1888

JUNE 16TH 1903

FROM THE RIVER TOWPATH AT THE BASE OF THE TOLLHOUSE CAN BE SEEN THE FLOOD MARKS THAT HAVE BEEN RECORDED THROUGHOUT THE YEARS, THE HIGHEST BEING THAT OF 1894

FROM A MAP OF 1808 - SHOWING THE TOLL HOUSE AND THE TURNPIKE GATES

Plate 16

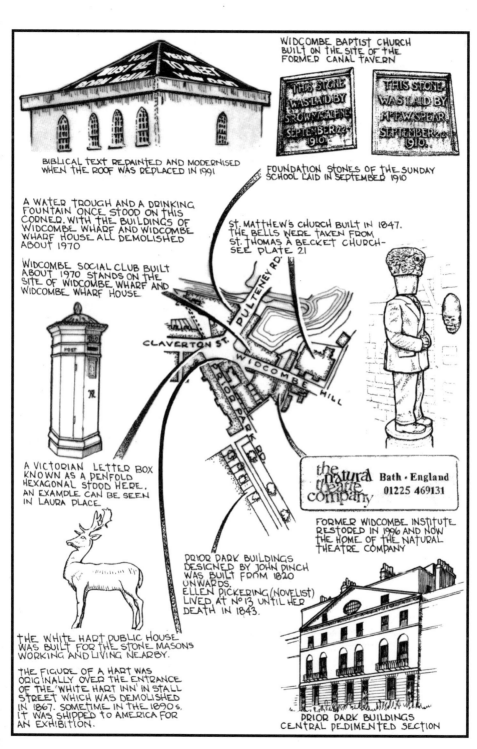

WIDCOMBE BAPTIST CHURCH BUILT ON THE SITE OF THE FORMER CANAL TAVERN

YOU MUST BE BORN AGAIN

THIS STONE WAS LAID BY S.ROW McALPINE SEPTEMBER 22 1910

THIS STONE WAS LAID BY M.F.W.SPEAR SEPTEMBER 22 1910

BIBLICAL TEXT REPAINTED AND MODERNISED WHEN THE ROOF WAS REPLACED IN 1991

FOUNDATION STONES OF THE SUNDAY SCHOOL LAID IN SEPTEMBER 1910

A WATER TROUGH AND A DRINKING FOUNTAIN ONCE STOOD ON THIS CORNER. WITH THE BUILDINGS OF WIDCOMBE WHARF AND WIDCOMBE WHARF HOUSE ALL DEMOLISHED ABOUT 1970

ST. MATTHEW'S CHURCH BUILT IN 1847. THE BELLS WERE TAKEN FROM ST. THOMAS À BECKET CHURCH- SEE PLATE 21

WIDCOMBE SOCIAL CLUB BUILT ABOUT 1970 STANDS ON THE SITE OF WIDCOMBE WHARF AND WIDCOMBE WHARF HOUSE

PULTENEY RD.

CLAVERTON ST.

WIDCOMBE HILL

PRIOR PARK RD

POST

A VICTORIAN LETTER BOX KNOWN AS A PENFOLD HEXAGONAL STOOD HERE. AN EXAMPLE CAN BE SEEN IN LAURA PLACE

the natural theatre company   Bath · England   01225 469131

FORMER WIDCOMBE INSTITUTE RESTORED IN 1996 AND NOW THE HOME OF THE NATURAL THEATRE COMPANY

PRIOR PARK BUILDINGS DESIGNED BY JOHN PINCH WAS BUILT FROM 1820 ONWARDS. ELLEN PICKERING (NOVELIST) LIVED AT No 13 UNTIL HER DEATH IN 1843.

THE WHITE HART PUBLIC HOUSE WAS BUILT FOR THE STONE MASONS WORKING AND LIVING NEARBY.

THE FIGURE OF A HART WAS ORIGINALLY OVER THE ENTRANCE OF THE 'WHITE HART INN' IN STALL STREET WHICH WAS DEMOLISHED IN 1867. SOMETIME IN THE 1890s IT WAS SHIPPED TO AMERICA FOR AN EXHIBITION.

PRIOR PARK BUILDINGS CENTRAL PEDIMENTED SECTION

Plate 17

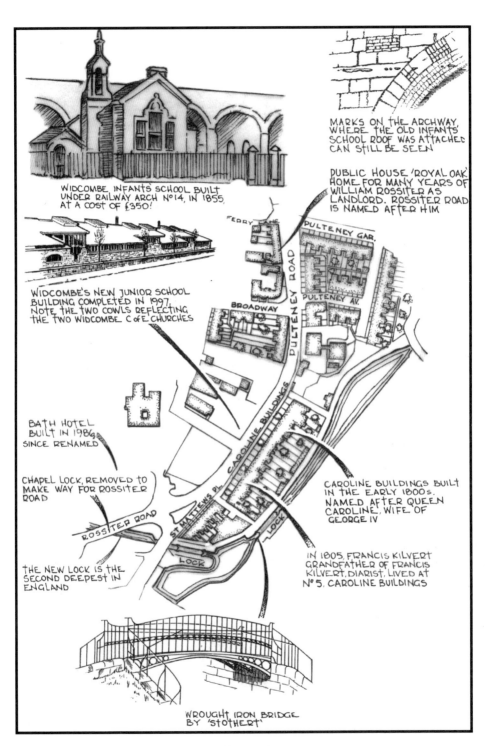

WIDCOMBE INFANTS SCHOOL BUILT UNDER RAILWAY ARCH Nº14, IN 1855, AT A COST OF £350!

MARKS ON THE ARCHWAY, WHERE THE OLD INFANTS SCHOOL ROOF WAS ATTACHED CAN STILL BE SEEN

PUBLIC HOUSE 'ROYAL OAK' HOME FOR MANY YEARS OF WILLIAM ROSSITER AS LANDLORD. ROSSITER ROAD IS NAMED AFTER HIM

WIDCOMBE'S NEW JUNIOR SCHOOL BUILDING COMPLETED IN 1997. NOTE THE TWO COWLS REFLECTING THE TWO WIDCOMBE C of E CHURCHES

FERRY LANE

PULTENEY GAR.

PULTENEY ROAD

PULTENEY AV.

BROADWAY

BATH HOTEL BUILT IN 1986, SINCE RENAMED

CAROLINE BUILDINGS

CHAPEL LOCK, REMOVED TO MAKE WAY FOR ROSSITER ROAD

ROSSITER ROAD

St MATTHEWS Pl

LOCK

CAROLINE BUILDINGS BUILT IN THE EARLY 1800s. NAMED AFTER QUEEN CAROLINE, WIFE OF GEORGE IV

THE NEW LOCK IS THE SECOND DEEPEST IN ENGLAND

LOCK

IN 1805, FRANCIS KILVERT GRANDFATHER OF FRANCIS KILVERT, DIARIST, LIVED AT Nº 5, CAROLINE BUILDINGS

WROUGHT IRON BRIDGE BY 'STOTHERT'

Plate 18

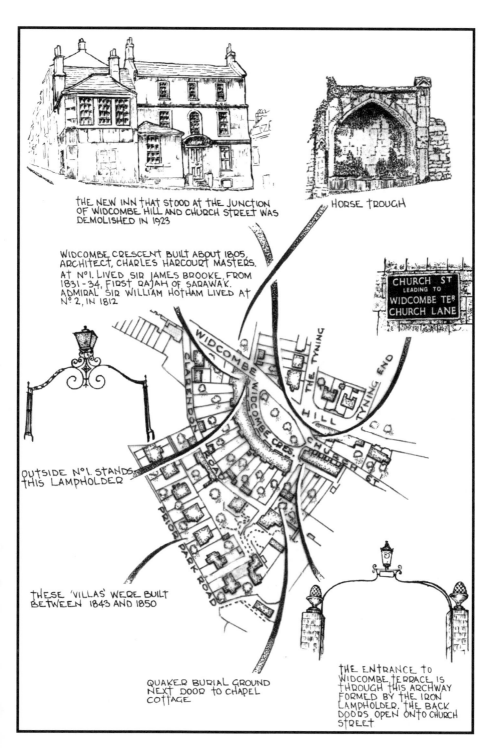

THE NEW INN THAT STOOD AT THE JUNCTION OF WIDCOMBE HILL AND CHURCH STREET WAS DEMOLISHED IN 1923

HORSE TROUGH

WIDCOMBE CRESCENT BUILT ABOUT 1805, ARCHITECT, CHARLES HARCOURT MASTERS. AT Nº1. LIVED SIR JAMES BROOKE, FROM 1831-34, FIRST RAJAH OF SARAWAK. ADMIRAL SIR WILLIAM HOTHAM LIVED AT Nº 2, IN 1812

CHURCH ST
LEADING TO
WIDCOMBE TERᴿ
CHURCH LANE

OUTSIDE Nº1. STANDS THIS LAMPHOLDER

THESE 'VILLAS' WERE BUILT BETWEEN 1843 AND 1850

QUAKER BURIAL GROUND NEXT DOOR TO CHAPEL COTTAGE

THE ENTRANCE TO WIDCOMBE TERRACE IS THROUGH THIS ARCHWAY FORMED BY THE IRON LAMPHOLDER. THE BACK DOORS OPEN ONTO CHURCH STREET

Plate 19

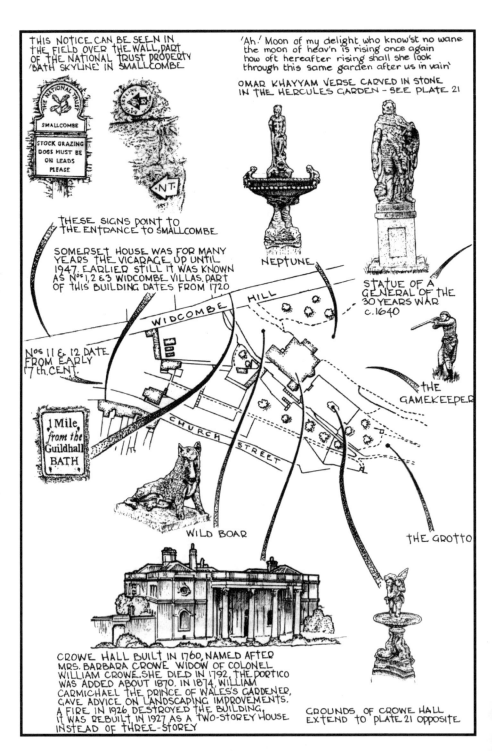

THIS NOTICE CAN BE SEEN IN THE FIELD OVER THE WALL, PART OF THE NATIONAL TRUST PROPERTY 'BATH SKYLINE' IN SMALLCOMBE

SMALLCOMBE

STOCK GRAZING
DOGS MUST BE
ON LEADS
PLEASE

N.T.

THESE SIGNS POINT TO THE ENTRANCE TO SMALLCOMBE

'Ah! Moon of my delight who know'st no wane
the moon of heav'n is rising once again
how oft hereafter rising shall she look
through this same garden after us in vain'

OMAR KHAYYAM VERSE CARVED IN STONE IN THE HERCULES GARDEN - SEE PLATE 21

NEPTUNE

STATUE OF A GENERAL OF THE 30 YEARS WAR c.1640

SOMERSET HOUSE WAS FOR MANY YEARS THE VICARAGE UP UNTIL 1947. EARLIER STILL IT WAS KNOWN AS Nos 1, 2 & 3 WIDCOMBE VILLAS. PART OF THIS BUILDING DATES FROM 1720

WIDCOMBE HILL

THE GAMEKEEPER

Nos 11 & 12 DATE FROM EARLY 17th CENT.

1 Mile
from the
Guildhall
BATH

CHURCH STREET

WILD BOAR

THE GROTTO

CROWE HALL BUILT IN 1760, NAMED AFTER MRS. BARBARA CROWE, WIDOW OF COLONEL WILLIAM CROWE. SHE DIED IN 1792. THE PORTICO WAS ADDED ABOUT 1870. IN 1874, WILLIAM CARMICHAEL THE PRINCE OF WALES'S GARDENER, GAVE ADVICE ON LANDSCAPING IMPROVEMENTS. A FIRE IN 1926 DESTROYED THE BUILDING, IT WAS REBUILT IN 1927 AS A TWO-STOREY HOUSE INSTEAD OF THREE-STOREY

GROUNDS OF CROWE HALL EXTEND TO PLATE 21 OPPOSITE

Plate 20

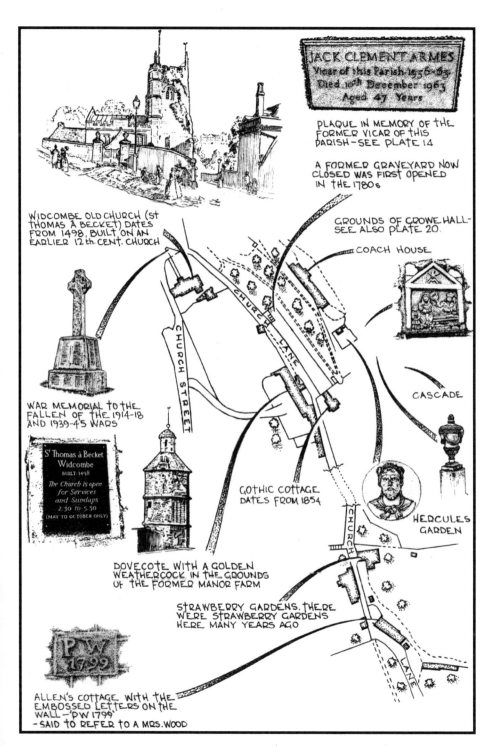

JACK CLEMENT ARMES
Vicar of this Parish 1956-63
Died 10th December 1963
Aged 47 Years

PLAQUE IN MEMORY OF THE FORMER VICAR OF THIS PARISH—SEE PLATE 14

A FORMER GRAVEYARD NOW CLOSED WAS FIRST OPENED IN THE 1780s

WIDCOMBE OLD CHURCH (St THOMAS À BECKET) DATES FROM 1498, BUILT ON AN EARLIER 12th. CENT. CHURCH

GROUNDS OF CROWE HALL—SEE ALSO PLATE 20.

COACH HOUSE

CHURCH LANE

CHURCH STREET

CASCADE

WAR MEMORIAL TO THE FALLEN OF THE 1914-18 AND 1939-45 WARS

St Thomas à Becket
Widcombe
BUILT 1498
The Church is open for Services on Sundays
2.30 to 5.30
(MAY TO OCTOBER ONLY)

GOTHIC COTTAGE DATES FROM 1854

CHURCH LANE

HERCULES GARDEN

DOVECOTE WITH A GOLDEN WEATHERCOCK IN THE GROUNDS OF THE FORMER MANOR FARM

STRAWBERRY GARDENS. THERE WERE STRAWBERRY GARDENS HERE MANY YEARS AGO

PW 1799

ALLEN'S COTTAGE WITH THE EMBOSSED LETTERS ON THE WALL—'PW 1799' - SAID TO REFER TO A MRS. WOOD

Plate 21

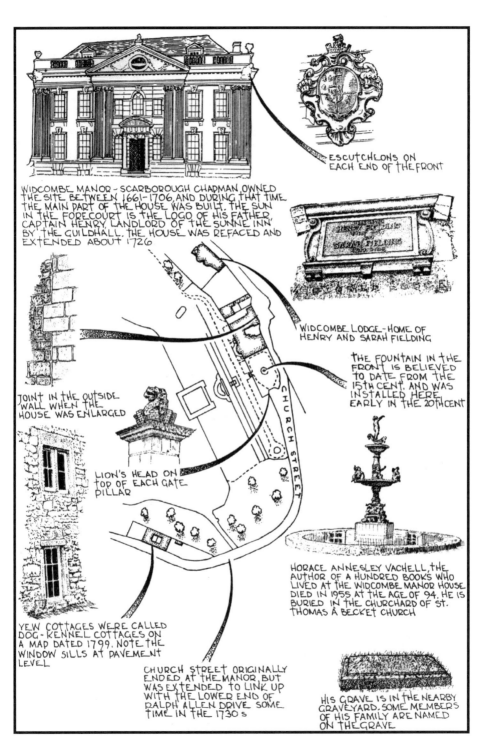

ESCUTCHEONS ON
EACH END OF THE FRONT

WIDCOMBE MANOR - SCARBOROUGH CHAPMAN OWNED
THE SITE BETWEEN 1661-1706, AND DURING THAT TIME
THE MAIN PART OF THE HOUSE WAS BUILT. THE SUN
IN THE FORECOURT IS THE LOGO OF HIS FATHER,
CAPTAIN HENRY, LANDLORD OF THE 'SUNNE INN'
BY THE GUILDHALL. THE HOUSE WAS REFACED AND
EXTENDED ABOUT 1726

WIDCOMBE LODGE - HOME OF
HENRY AND SARAH FIELDING

JOINT IN THE OUTSIDE
WALL WHEN THE
HOUSE WAS ENLARGED

THE FOUNTAIN IN THE
FRONT IS BELIEVED
TO DATE FROM THE
15TH CENT. AND WAS
INSTALLED HERE
EARLY IN THE 20TH CENT

LION'S HEAD ON
TOP OF EACH GATE
PILLAR

HORACE ANNESLEY VACHELL, THE
AUTHOR OF A HUNDRED BOOKS WHO
LIVED AT THE WIDCOMBE MANOR HOUSE
DIED IN 1955 AT THE AGE OF 94. HE IS
BURIED IN THE CHURCHARD OF ST.
THOMAS À BECKET CHURCH

YEW COTTAGES WERE CALLED
DOG-KENNEL COTTAGES ON
A MAP DATED 1799. NOTE THE
WINDOW SILLS AT PAVEMENT
LEVEL

CHURCH STREET ORIGINALLY
ENDED AT THE MANOR, BUT
WAS EXTENDED TO LINK UP
WITH THE LOWER END OF
RALPH ALLEN DRIVE SOME
TIME IN THE 1730s

HIS GRAVE IS IN THE NEARBY
GRAVEYARD. SOME MEMBERS
OF HIS FAMILY ARE NAMED
ON THE GRAVE

Plate 22

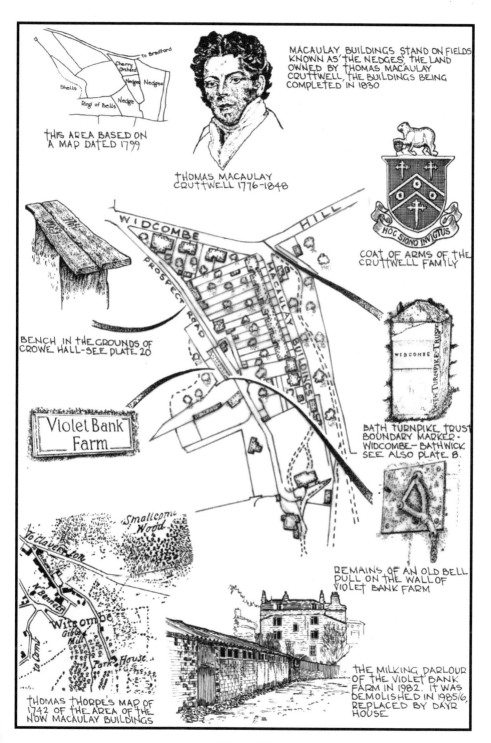

THIS AREA BASED ON A MAP DATED 1799

MACAULAY BUILDINGS STAND ON FIELDS KNOWN AS THE NEDGES, THE LAND OWNED BY THOMAS MACAULAY CRUTTWELL, THE BUILDINGS BEING COMPLETED IN 1830

THOMAS MACAULAY CRUTTWELL 1776-1848

HOC SIGNO INVICTUS

COAT OF ARMS OF THE CRUTTWELL FAMILY

BENCH IN THE GROUNDS OF CROWE HALL-SEE PLATE 20

Violet Bank Farm

WIDCOMBE

BATH TURNPIKE TRUST

BATH TURNPIKE TRUST BOUNDARY MARKER - WIDCOMBE — BATHWICK SEE ALSO PLATE 8.

REMAINS OF AN OLD BELL PULL ON THE WALL OF VIOLET BANK FARM

THOMAS THORPE'S MAP OF 1742 OF THE AREA OF THE NOW MACAULAY BUILDINGS

THE MILKING PARLOUR OF THE VIOLET BANK FARM IN 1982. IT WAS DEMOLISHED IN 1985/6, REPLACED BY DAYR HOUSE

Plate 23

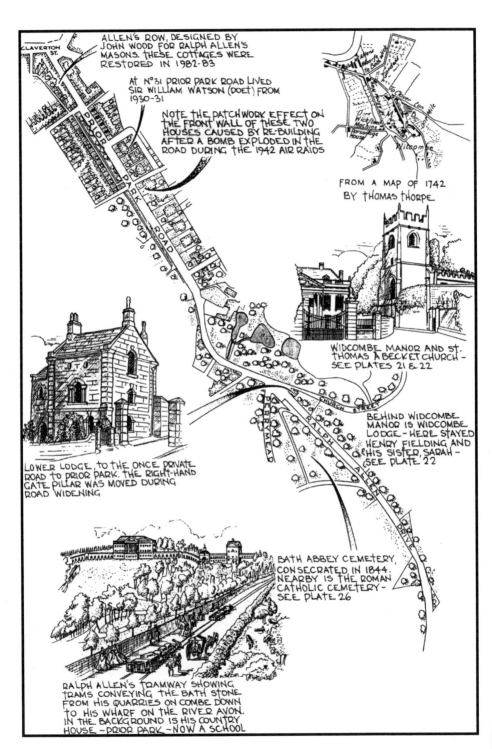

ALLEN'S ROW, DESIGNED BY JOHN WOOD FOR RALPH ALLEN'S MASONS. THESE COTTAGES WERE RESTORED IN 1982-83

AT N°31 PRIOR PARK ROAD LIVED SIR WILLIAM WATSON (POET) FROM 1930-31

NOTE THE PATCHWORK EFFECT ON THE FRONT WALL OF THESE TWO HOUSES CAUSED BY RE-BUILDING AFTER A BOMB EXPLODED IN THE ROAD DURING THE 1942 AIR RAIDS

FROM A MAP OF 1742 BY THOMAS THORPE

WIDCOMBE MANOR AND ST. THOMAS À BECKET CHURCH – SEE PLATES 21 & 22

BEHIND WIDCOMBE MANOR IS WIDCOMBE LODGE – HERE STAYED HENRY FIELDING AND HIS SISTER, SARAH – SEE PLATE 22

LOWER LODGE, TO THE ONCE PRIVATE ROAD TO PRIOR PARK. THE RIGHT-HAND GATE PILLAR WAS MOVED DURING ROAD WIDENING

BATH ABBEY CEMETERY, CONSECRATED IN 1844. NEARBY IS THE ROMAN CATHOLIC CEMETERY – SEE PLATE 26

RALPH ALLEN'S TRAMWAY SHOWING TRAMS CONVEYING THE BATH STONE FROM HIS QUARRIES ON COMBE DOWN TO HIS WHARF ON THE RIVER AVON. IN THE BACKGROUND IS HIS COUNTRY HOUSE – PRIOR PARK – NOW A SCHOOL

Plate 24

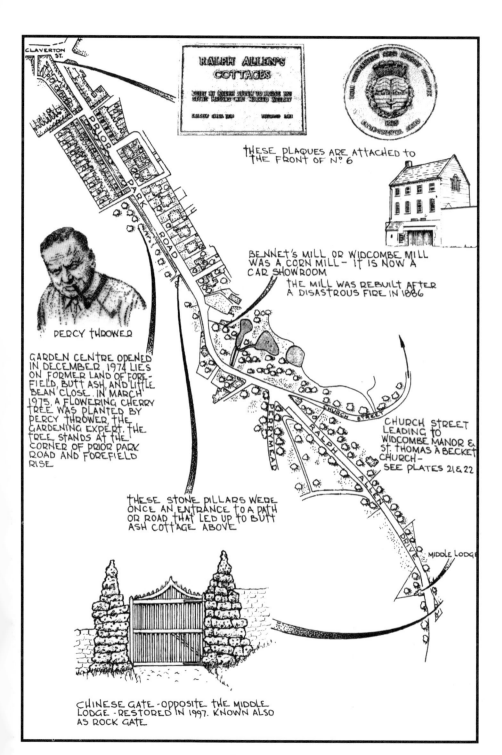

CLAVERTON ST.

PRIOR PARK ROAD

RALPH ALLEN'S COTTAGES

THESE PLAQUES ARE ATTACHED TO THE FRONT OF Nº 6

BENNET'S MILL OR WIDCOMBE MILL WAS A CORN MILL – IT IS NOW A CAR SHOWROOM

THE MILL WAS REBUILT AFTER A DISASTROUS FIRE IN 1886

PERCY THROWER

GARDEN CENTRE OPENED IN DECEMBER 1974 LIES ON FORMER LAND OF FORE-FIELD, BUTT ASH, AND LITTLE BEAN CLOSE. IN MARCH 1975, A FLOWERING CHERRY TREE WAS PLANTED BY PERCY THROWER, THE GARDENING EXPERT. THE TREE STANDS AT THE CORNER OF PRIOR PARK ROAD AND FOREFIELD RISE

PERRYMEAD

RALPH ALLEN

CHURCH STREET

CHURCH STREET LEADING TO WIDCOMBE MANOR & ST. THOMAS A BECKET CHURCH – SEE PLATES 21 & 22

THESE STONE PILLARS WERE ONCE AN ENTRANCE TO A PATH OR ROAD THAT LED UP TO BUTT ASH COTTAGE ABOVE

DRIVE

MIDDLE LODGE

CHINESE GATE – OPPOSITE THE MIDDLE LODGE – RESTORED IN 1997. KNOWN ALSO AS ROCK GATE

Plate 25

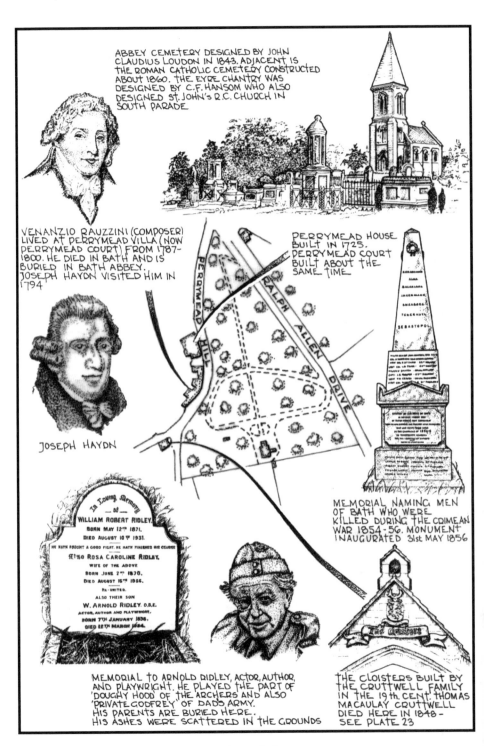

ABBEY CEMETERY DESIGNED BY JOHN CLAUDIUS LOUDON IN 1843. ADJACENT IS THE ROMAN CATHOLIC CEMETERY CONSTRUCTED ABOUT 1860. THE EYRE CHANTRY WAS DESIGNED BY C.F. HANSOM WHO ALSO DESIGNED ST. JOHN'S R.C. CHURCH IN SOUTH PARADE

VENANZIO RAUZZINI (COMPOSER) LIVED AT PERRYMEAD VILLA (NOW PERRYMEAD COURT) FROM 1787-1800. HE DIED IN BATH AND IS BURIED IN BATH ABBEY. JOSEPH HAYDN VISITED HIM IN 1794

JOSEPH HAYDN

PERRYMEAD HOUSE BUILT IN 1725. PERRYMEAD COURT BUILT ABOUT THE SAME TIME

PERRYMEAD HILL

RALPH ALLEN DRIVE

In Loving Memory
— of —
WILLIAM ROBERT RIDLEY.
BORN MAY 12th 1871.
DIED AUGUST 10th 1931.
HE HATH FOUGHT A GOOD FIGHT. HE HATH FINISHED HIS COURSE.
Also ROSA CAROLINE RIDLEY.
WIFE OF THE ABOVE
BORN JUNE 2nd 1870.
DIED AUGUST 16th 1956.
RE-UNITED.
ALSO THEIR SON
W. ARNOLD RIDLEY. O.B.E.
ACTOR, AUTHOR AND PLAYWRIGHT.
BORN 7th JANUARY 1896.
DIED 12th MARCH 1984.

MEMORIAL NAMING MEN OF BATH WHO WERE KILLED DURING THE CRIMEAN WAR 1854-56. MONUMENT INAUGURATED 31st MAY 1856

MEMORIAL TO ARNOLD RIDLEY, ACTOR, AUTHOR, AND PLAYWRIGHT. HE PLAYED THE PART OF 'DOUGHY HOOD' OF THE ARCHERS AND ALSO 'PRIVATE GODFREY' OF DAD'S ARMY. HIS PARENTS ARE BURIED HERE. HIS ASHES WERE SCATTERED IN THE GROUNDS

THE CLOISTERS BUILT BY THE CRUTTWELL FAMILY IN THE 19th. CENT. THOMAS MACAULAY CRUTTWELL DIED HERE IN 1848 - SEE PLATE 23

Plate 26

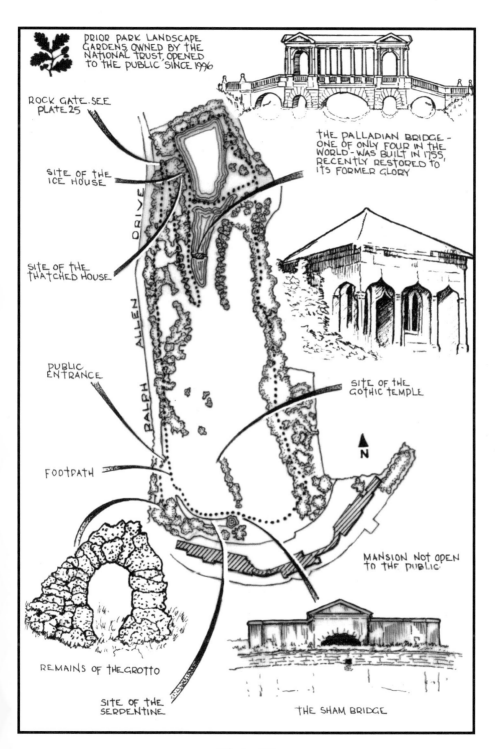

PRIOR PARK LANDSCAPE GARDENS, OWNED BY THE NATIONAL TRUST, OPENED TO THE PUBLIC SINCE 1996

ROCK GATE. SEE PLATE 25

THE PALLADIAN BRIDGE - ONE OF ONLY FOUR IN THE WORLD - WAS BUILT IN 1755, RECENTLY RESTORED TO ITS FORMER GLORY

SITE OF THE ICE HOUSE

SITE OF THE THATCHED HOUSE

RALPH ALLEN DRIVE

PUBLIC ENTRANCE

SITE OF THE GOTHIC TEMPLE

N

FOOTPATH

MANSION NOT OPEN TO THE PUBLIC

REMAINS OF THE GROTTO

SITE OF THE SERPENTINE

THE SHAM BRIDGE

Plate 27

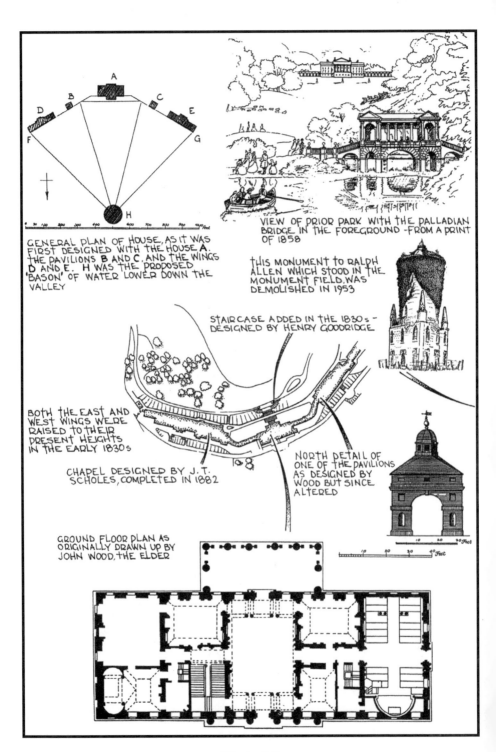

GENERAL PLAN OF HOUSE, AS IT WAS FIRST DESIGNED WITH THE HOUSE A. THE PAVILIONS B AND C, AND THE WINGS D AND E. H WAS THE PROPOSED 'BASON' OF WATER LOWER DOWN THE VALLEY

VIEW OF PRIOR PARK WITH THE PALLADIAN BRIDGE IN THE FOREGROUND - FROM A PRINT OF 1858

THIS MONUMENT TO RALPH ALLEN WHICH STOOD IN THE MONUMENT FIELD, WAS DEMOLISHED IN 1953

STAIRCASE ADDED IN THE 1830s - DESIGNED BY HENRY GOODRIDGE

BOTH THE EAST AND WEST WINGS WERE RAISED TO THEIR PRESENT HEIGHTS IN THE EARLY 1830s

CHAPEL DESIGNED BY J. T. SCHOLES, COMPLETED IN 1882

NORTH DETAIL OF ONE OF THE PAVILIONS AS DESIGNED BY WOOD BUT SINCE ALTERED

GROUND FLOOR PLAN AS ORIGINALLY DRAWN UP BY JOHN WOOD, THE ELDER

Plate 28

NORTH ELEVATION OF MR.ALLEN'S HOUSE, IN THE 'WIDCOMB OF
CAMALODUNUM', NEAR BATH, WITH THE WINDOWS DRESSED
ACCORDING TO THE ORIGINAL DESIGN — FROM JOHN WOOD'S
'ESSAY TOWARDS A DESCRIPTION OF BATH' 1749

RALPH ALLEN FROM A PAINTING
BY THOMAS HUDSON 1751.
THIS PORTRAIT HANGS IN THE
PUMP ROOM

SOME OF RALPH ALLEN'S GUESTS DURING
HIS 20 YEARS AT PRIOR PARK WERE —
HENRY FIELDING
THOMAS GAINSBOROUGH
DAVID GARRICK
WILLIAM HOARE
ALEXANDER POPE
JAMES QUIN
SAMUEL RICHARDSON
BISHOP WARBURTON

PART OF MAP MARKED OUT AS
LOTS IN PREPARATION FOR
SALE IN 1856

Plate 29

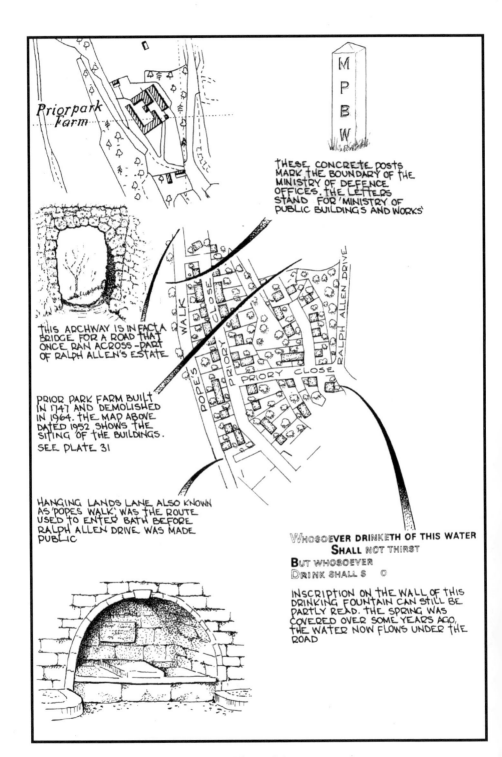

Priorpark Farm

M
P
B
W

THESE CONCRETE POSTS
MARK THE BOUNDARY OF THE
MINISTRY OF DEFENCE
OFFICES. THE LETTERS
STAND FOR 'MINISTRY OF
PUBLIC BUILDINGS AND WORKS'

THIS ARCHWAY IS IN FACT A
BRIDGE FOR A ROAD THAT
ONCE RAN ACROSS PART
OF RALPH ALLEN'S ESTATE

PRIOR PARK FARM BUILT
IN 1747 AND DEMOLISHED
IN 1964. THE MAP ABOVE
DATED 1952 SHOWS THE
SITING OF THE BUILDINGS.
SEE PLATE 31

HANGING LANDS LANE ALSO KNOWN
AS 'POPES WALK', WAS THE ROUTE
USED TO ENTER BATH BEFORE
RALPH ALLEN DRIVE WAS MADE
PUBLIC

WALK

POPES

PRIORY

CLOSE

PRIORY CLOSE

RALPH ALLEN DRIVE

WHOSOEVER DRINKETH OF THIS WATER
SHALL NOT THIRST
BUT WHOSOEVER
DRINK SHALL S   O

INSCRIPTION ON THE WALL OF THIS
DRINKING FOUNTAIN CAN STILL BE
PARTLY READ. THE SPRING WAS
COVERED OVER SOME YEARS AGO,
THE WATER NOW FLOWS UNDER THE
ROAD

Plate 30

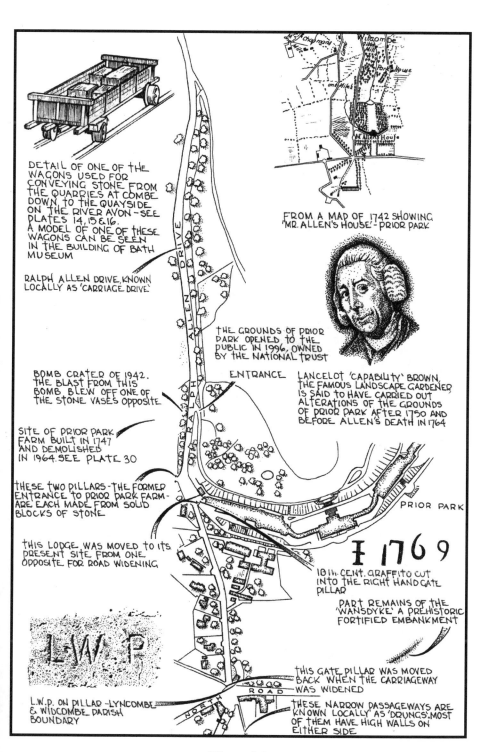

DETAIL OF ONE OF THE WAGONS USED FOR CONVEYING STONE FROM THE QUARRIES AT COMBE DOWN, TO THE QUAYSIDE ON THE RIVER AVON – SEE PLATES 14, 15 & 16.
A MODEL OF ONE OF THESE WAGONS CAN BE SEEN IN THE BUILDING OF BATH MUSEUM

RALPH ALLEN DRIVE, KNOWN LOCALLY AS 'CARRIAGE DRIVE'

FROM A MAP OF 1742 SHOWING 'MR. ALLEN'S HOUSE' – PRIOR PARK

THE GROUNDS OF PRIOR PARK OPENED TO THE PUBLIC IN 1996, OWNED BY THE NATIONAL TRUST

ENTRANCE

LANCELOT 'CAPABILITY' BROWN, THE FAMOUS LANDSCAPE GARDENER IS SAID TO HAVE CARRIED OUT ALTERATIONS OF THE GROUNDS OF PRIOR PARK AFTER 1750 AND BEFORE ALLEN'S DEATH IN 1764

BOMB CRATER OF 1942. THE BLAST FROM THIS BOMB BLEW OFF ONE OF THE STONE VASES OPPOSITE

SITE OF PRIOR PARK FARM BUILT IN 1747 AND DEMOLISHED IN 1964. SEE PLATE 30

THESE TWO PILLARS – THE FORMER ENTRANCE TO PRIOR PARK FARM – ARE EACH MADE FROM SOLID BLOCKS OF STONE

THIS LODGE WAS MOVED TO ITS PRESENT SITE FROM ONE OPPOSITE FOR ROAD WIDENING

PRIOR PARK

Ŧ 1769

18TH CENT. GRAFFITO CUT INTO THE RIGHT HAND GATE PILLAR

PART REMAINS OF THE 'WANSDYKE' A PREHISTORIC FORTIFIED EMBANKMENT

THIS GATE PILLAR WAS MOVED BACK WHEN THE CARRIAGEWAY WAS WIDENED

L.W.P. ON PILLAR – LYNCOMBE & WIDCOMBE PARISH BOUNDARY

THESE NARROW PASSAGEWAYS ARE KNOWN LOCALLY AS 'DRUNGS'. MOST OF THEM HAVE HIGH WALLS ON EITHER SIDE

Plate 31

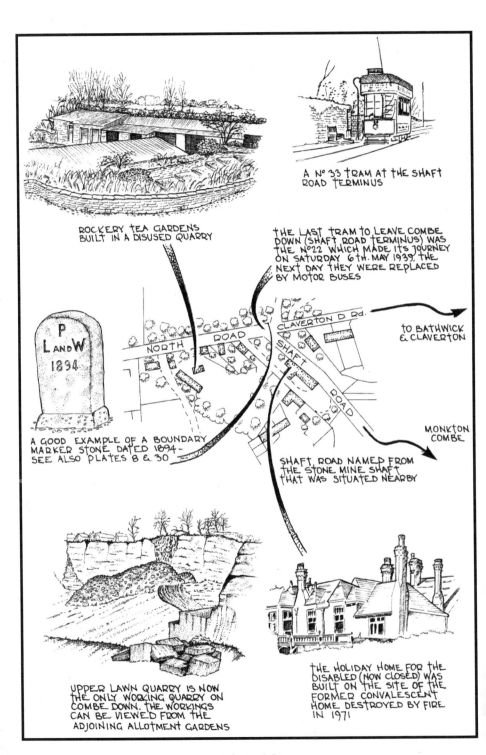

ROCKERY TEA GARDENS
BUILT IN A DISUSED QUARRY

A Nº 33 TRAM AT THE SHAFT
ROAD TERMINUS

THE LAST TRAM TO LEAVE COMBE
DOWN (SHAFT ROAD TERMINUS) WAS
THE Nº22 WHICH MADE ITS JOURNEY
ON SATURDAY 6TH. MAY 1939. THE
NEXT DAY THEY WERE REPLACED
BY MOTOR BUSES

P
L AND W
1894

NORTH ROAD

CLAVERTON D. Rd.

SHAFT ROAD

TO BATHWICK
& CLAVERTON

MONKTON
COMBE

A GOOD EXAMPLE OF A BOUNDARY
MARKER STONE DATED 1894 -
SEE ALSO PLATES 8 & 30

SHAFT ROAD NAMED FROM
THE STONE MINE SHAFT
THAT WAS SITUATED NEARBY

UPPER LAWN QUARRY IS NOW
THE ONLY WORKING QUARRY ON
COMBE DOWN. THE WORKINGS
CAN BE VIEWED FROM THE
ADJOINING ALLOTMENT GARDENS

THE HOLIDAY HOME FOR THE
DISABLED (NOW CLOSED) WAS
BUILT ON THE SITE OF THE
FORMER CONVALESCENT
HOME DESTROYED BY FIRE
IN 1971

Plate 32